T0413869

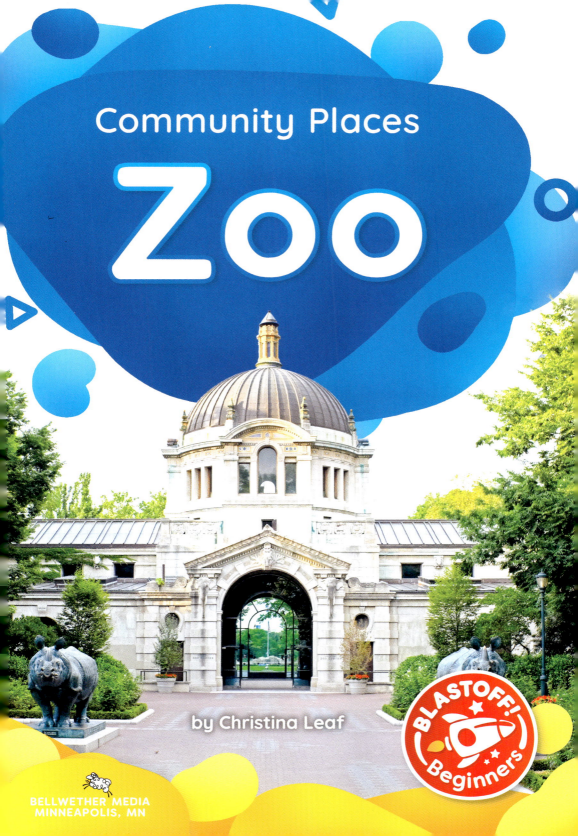

Community Places

Zoo

by Christina Leaf

BELLWETHER MEDIA
MINNEAPOLIS, MN

BLASTOFF!
Beginners

Blastoff! Beginners are developed by literacy experts and educators to meet the needs of early readers. These engaging informational texts support young children as they begin reading about their world. Through simple language and high frequency words paired with crisp, colorful photos, Blastoff! Beginners launch young readers into the universe of independent reading.

Blastoff! Universe

Reading Level

Grade K

Grades 1-3

Grade 4

Sight Words in This Book 🔍

about	has	look	them
all	have	many	these
are	in	of	they
at	is	see	this
for	it	some	to
go	like	the	we

This edition first published in 2023 by Bellwether Media, Inc.

No part of this publication may be reproduced in whole or in part without written permission of the publisher. For information regarding permission, write to Bellwether Media, Inc., Attention: Permissions Department, 6012 Blue Circle Drive, Minnetonka, MN 55343.

Library of Congress Cataloging-in-Publication Data

Names: Leaf, Christina, author.
Title: Zoo / by Christina Leaf.
Description: Minneapolis, MN : Bellwether Media, Inc., 2023. | Series: Blastoff! beginners : Community places | Includes bibliographical references and index. | Audience: Ages 4-7 | Audience: Grades K-1
Identifiers: LCCN 2022036349 (print) | LCCN 2022036350 (ebook) | ISBN9798886870992 (library binding) | ISBN 9798886872255 (ebook)
Subjects: LCSH: Zoos--Juvenile literature.
Classification: LCC QL76 .L43 2023 (print) | LCC QL76 (ebook) | DDC 590.73--dc23/eng/20220818
LC record available at https://lccn.loc.gov/2022036349
LC ebook record available at https://lccn.loc.gov/2022036350

Editor: Rebecca Sabelko   Designer: Gabriel Hilger

Printed in the United States of America, North Mankato, MN.

Table of Contents

At the Zoo!

Look at all
the animals.
We are at
the zoo!

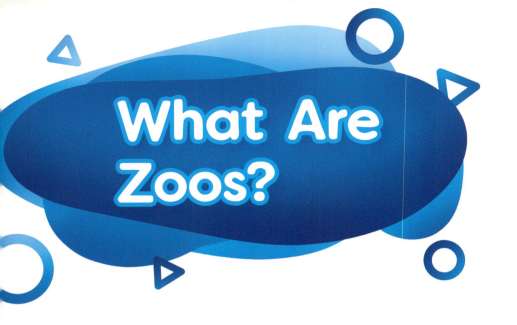

What Are Zoos?

Zoos are
fun places!
They have many
kinds of animals.

Visitors go to see the animals. Some workers study the animals.

worker

A Zoo Visit

Animals live in **enclosures**. These look like wild animal homes.

enclosure

Zookeepers care for the animals. They feed them.

zookeeper

13

Zookeepers give talks. Visitors learn about animals!

This is the **aviary**.
Birds fly around!

aviary

This is the
aquarium.
It has many fish.

aquarium

This is the
petting zoo.
We love the zoo!

petting zoo

21

Zoo Facts

At the Zoo

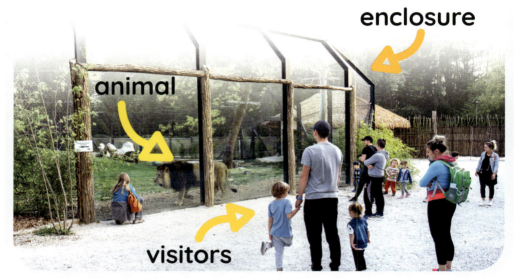

enclosure

animal

visitors

What Happens at a Zoo?

study animals

care for animals

give talks

Glossary

aquarium

the part of a zoo with many fish

aviary

the part of a zoo with many birds

enclosures

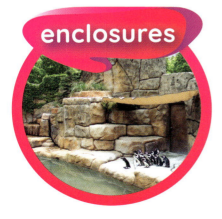

areas in zoos where the animals live

zookeepers

people who care for animals in zoos

To Learn More

ON THE WEB

FACTSURFER

Factsurfer.com gives you a safe, fun way to find more information.

1. Go to www.factsurfer.com.

2. Enter "zoo" into the search box and click 🔍.

3. Select your book cover to see a list of related content.

Index

The images in this book are reproduced through the courtesy of: a katz, front cover; Luis Louro, p. 3; tiburonstudios, pp. 4-5; Catarina Williams, pp. 6-7; Deni Williams, pp. 8-9; Hayk_Shalunts, pp. 10-11; Evannovostro, pp. 12-13; Vincentstthomas, pp. 14-15; Rudolf Ernst/ Getty Images, p. 16; RaymondAsiaPhotography/ Alamy, pp. 16-17; ROSLAN RAHMAN / Contributor/ Getty Images, pp. 18-19; Baby2M, pp. 20-21; Bizi88, p. 22 (at the zoo); Kirk Fisher, p. 22 (study animals); Hel080808, p. 22 (care for animals); Orion Media Group, p. 22 (give talks); Maria Sbytova, p. 23 (aquarium); Yane Yulliane, p. 23 (aviary); Eclectic_Fishbowl, p. 23 (enclosures); Ehw258, p. 23 (zookeepers).